Deep
in
Time

by Cora Greenhill

Also by Cora Greenhill: Dreadful Work (1989)

ISBN 0 9514826 1 0

© 1999 Cora Greenhill (poems and photographs)
© (all other artwork) the artists

Published by
Dreadful Work Press,
9, The Windses, Grindleford, Hope Valley, S32 2HY.
email: cora@thirteenthmoon.demon.co.uk
website: http://www.thirteenthmoon.demon.co.uk

Design and production: Dick Richardson, Country Books, Little Longstone DE45 1NN

Distribution and orders to: Dick Richardson, Country Books, Little Longstone DE45 1NN

For my parents,
who took me to live on the land, set me free,
and taught me to love words.

With deep thanks to Gabrielle Roth for the privilege of being her student for so many years and the immeasurable gift of the dance; and to all who have supported, encouraged and inspired me for so long: you know who you are!

Acknowledgements: some of these poems were previously published (or excerpted) in the following publications:

Writing Women (1994), Staple (22 and 24), The New Writer (1996), Cahoots Magazine, Lancashire LitFest Anthologies (1995 & 97), Fire (1998 & 99); We'moon (1994,97,98,99) Writing for our Lives (CA 1995 &98)
and in the following books: If Not a Mother (Souvenir Press), The West in Her Eye (Pyramid Press), In Her Mind's Eye (Pyramid Press), Dancing in the Dangerzone (Making Waves), Nailing Colours (Crocus),Sweat Your Prayers by Gabrielle Roth (Tarcher Putman).

CONTENTS

Deep
in
Time

by Cora Greenhill

Artwork:
Drawings by Pauline Rignall
(unless otherwise attributed.)
Photography
(including front cover)
by Cora Greenhill

Waiting for Change

She has no shape or colour
she merges with everything
absorbs the unremarkable
sinks into clay
part of the ordinary
unobserved day.

She waits
like the grainy hollow in the stone
for rain
and holds it
till the work of creation
ferments in her body.

The role of Mr Animus in producing a poem

When it first comes out
a blurt scrawled on the page
all gangly like a new wet calf
all wobbly
I'm not intrigued at all
I turn the page
can't be doing with it
would orphan the weakling
feel no connection
certainly no commitment
to training and feeding
– it needs so much of me
to survive.

What we need then
is a good farmer to arrive
a tough rough gentle
husbandman.
He'll use his big spade hands
to turn my disinterested
heavy head
towards the trembling waif,
make me see it, sniff it.
He'll give me a bit of encouragement
say my name
fuss me a bit.

Finally, I may lick it
taste it
and with a tingling rush in the udder
own it.

Night lines

I need a new kind of poem catcher
for these easy coming lines
that glide over pages

like pale cats
scaling fishboats
on this moon-bleached shore.

For when the barmen report
for their night shift at sea
loading tackle and lamps,

and the outboard's whining saw
drives into the lake-deep night
they slip away like dreams.

Rachael Levine

Differences

I crawl in fields of clay among the legs of men
lifting nests of purties* clean as eggs.
The boys get half a crown and I get sixpence.
I don't understand the difference. It isn't fair.
And the men set snares for rabbits and boys know where.

I ride in front of farmers' sons on tractors.
My arms are smooth but theirs are rough with hair.
I feel their squidgy things through overalls:
I'd always known they're different down there.
But men set snares for rabbits and boys know where.

We climb the high-stacked hay bales to the rafters.
The barn is dark but streaked with gold up here.
We make a nest and hide, trapping our laughter.
No fur is silkier than this new hair.
In here with me, you are not one of them:
Our fingers feel each other on a softly swelling stem.

But still, out there, when men set snares for rabbits
you know where.

* *Ulster dialect for potatoes.*

Harvesting Long Meadow

(I heard them say it will be cut to-morrow
rolled in black plastic tubes.
Too many flowers make it poor for fodder:
they'll harvest earlier another year.)

The evening sky is finger-painted
egg-brown and pigeon-grey.
A sheet of mist
hung from the tree line
hides the valley.

It is below the sheep slope
where the path is muddy
and the stink of hawthorn cuts the air
that I see a child of neither sex,
wading brown bogwater
spiked with seeded rushes
metalled marigolds
and quilts of cuckoo flowers
– a distant place
where a soul could stretch awake.

For here in henna light
that trails the setting sun
a scarlet haze of sorrel floats
above the heavy-headed crop
speckled with buttercups, clover, speedwell, campion and vetch.
Rushes, plantain, horsetail, edge the path
and clear blue eyebright sparkles in low grass.
Stichwort and wild parsley foam along the hedge
– the curd, the cream, the thick scum –

and a white moon slipping from under Froggat's brow
catches the pallor of a single cuckoo flower.

Gone with the Fairies

I recognise the way, though the hedges are lower,
the bends less sharp, the hills less steep,
than the road that hurled us from our bikes
paring the skin off my knees in shapes
that became pale but permanent
as if scars were in my genes.

This landscape marked me,
indelibly as those who brought me here from England
ensuring I would always find my home
where I was stranger.

I slow down the hire car
receiving curious glances from children
in a well-groomed garden
where I remembered wet meadow.
I take in ribbed concrete driveway
swerving between new walls...
and five bar iron gates.
Then their father, a policeman it later turns out,
wonders if he can help.

Strangers still don't pass unmarked here then –
the road still leads to nowhere
but the bogs of Bin Mountain
(where the turf was cut
and we perched on lurching towers of it
behind tractors, all the way down the bray.)

In the modern kitchen
his wife brings wrapped chocolate biscuits
arranged in a basket, with tea,
reminding me of Greek hospitality.
(We used to get big split potatoes
smeared with scum from the peat-reddened pot
with salt, from our neighbours' kitchens.)

They talk of the new prosperity, and the troubles since I left,
(but they'd started already then, with border skirmishes,
and I don't let on
my landscape was more like a bearded terrorist
than a clean-shaven policeman.

We knew the shortcuts across the burn
before these solid folk built fences.
The hedges dripping berries reached for you
catching your arms in briars and dog rose thorns
drawing beads of blood.
Your foot could sink among the spiky rushes
your wellingtons fill with slime.
The toes of my friend, fostered, too poor for socks,
had black tide-marks nearly as permanent as scars.

We'd speculated on the fairy rings,
dour children touched to the core
by the rough magic of this uncouth land.
We lit fires at Easter, stole eggs to boil,
hid in hollows deep in sea-green ferns.
and high in hay-filled barns.

We'd learnt a wary toughness
but we weren't prepared
when the farmers set fire
to the bright uncontrollable gorse
threatening our hoard
of miniscule strawberries beneath the banks.
And when the tree-high machines
ripped up our narrow red bray
scorching the air with smoke and hot asphalt
oozing tar to trap grasshoppers
and leaving a proper flat surface...

we stood in the silence that evening,
shivering at the cold
prospect of wide open futures, of change,

and you, my ragged friend,
uttered your question
with a shocking, precocious authority,
'They ruined it, did they?')

They did, and the nice policeman thinks
you – or your brother – got into trouble
and died.

My grandmother's bread tins

These could be museum pieces.
They're not moulded or stainless,
but rivetted together where the thin metal meets,
the black steel bent and folded.
The loaves always leave them clean.

As I handle them
I see your kitchen hands greasing them again:
arthritic knuckles and two and a half fingers missing
on the right, sliced off in the munitions factory
you worked in during the war.
You'd hold the loaf to your apron
with the heel of your right hand
as you pulled the knife with your left.

There was nothing you couldn't do in the house,
even play the piano,
but it had been a hard school.
As I grew older you sometimes spoke
of the tears you'd shed over washing
and scrubbing and baking
and holding and feeding the baby
all with one good hand.
It was a wonder you'd got a husband at all,
they would have said, with so many able women
and fewer and fewer men.

You took it to heart:
I remember him throned in his leather armchair
that gleamed like the dining table under its chenille wraps
and the great double basses he'd played
(once aboard The Queen Mary).

He still had his yorkshire and gravy
before the rest of his dinner
and my mother recounts
how they would get bread and dripping
while he'd got the end of the roast.

She also says you riled him
with your ignorant religion,
and playing hymns on the piano
out of tune. My mother
doesn't mince her words:
her contempt cuts deep.

You blamed the shell-shock
not the men
for spattering their sensitivity
like shrapnel round the house.
And you still got out a tin of spam or ham
if we brought a boyfriend to tea.
The belief had outlasted
two sonless generations:
a man needs his meat.

At eighty
you were still playing hymns,
were a dab hand at whist.
The habit of baking your own
lived on to the end:
there were scones and curd tarts
in the tins when they took you away.

You weren't the mother my mother deserved:
her mind would voyage far
from the kitchen and church door.
And when my own baking is praised
I can still feel demeaned
feeling her frustration
even now unforgiving,
snapping at those hands that fed her
conflating the broad hearth
with narrowness of mind.

My mother is proud of inheriting
her father's perfect pitch,
and buys sliced bread.

The Dark of Red Returning

1. *Waxing*

Down there
is dangerous as hell.

Red flowed from her
black red
bright red
stopping and starting.
Right red or wrong red?

Mother,
stormy in lakes of pain
womb gone
dead to her.

Toilet paper hardened in lumps
rubbing her raw
sore lips down there

but worse, it slipped
became a bump
in the back of serge knickers
threatening exposure.

Hot red shame
simmered.

Stiff, brown, gussets
won't come clean.
Knuckles blister and bleed
at the feverish scrubbing.

But between the blood times
the muddy-crust-between-the-legs times
she sharpened the edges
of dangerous desire
alone
piercing a fearsome pleasure
with fingers
and other things.
Only half hidden
she finds smooth stones and stalks
or sits astride big field gates
boughs of trees

casting around
counting
knowing
she would come

become
a woman
on her own,
only half hiding.

(Around that time
she was saved.
Joined the Scripture Union.
Looked for crosses in cracked plaster
on the walls
wanting signs and fearing punishment)

Valerie T Bechtol

2. *Fullness*

The signs circled ceaselessly
reliable as tides.
They spun the days and weeks into wheels
reeled out
the rhythms of a beaded thread:

this blessed curse we lived with
this inconvenient summons
this regular and unrelenting
inner call to prayer.

The ache of blood relief
the out-breath of the womb
the slackening
the letting go
the making way
withdrawing

was all the way of travelling
I, we, women, knew.
Even after birthing
the red returned so soon:
blood, milk, sperm
all mixed in a new brew.

3. *Waning*

Red-faced, foolish,
warning lights flash:
woman in her fertile years no more.
And they see.
They'll say
not her – she's – changed.
No denial of age now.
('Are you grey yet? Under the henna?')
No disguising *this* colour change.

Red anytime now
wrongtime, between blood times
black red
dead red
killing desire.

No cycle returning
reliable as tides.
Soon, no red time
no womb time
no womb?

Doctors, deaf to me
mutter, 'Dysfunctional bleeding.'
Add, 'We could take it out,
along with the fibroids –
save trouble later.'

Red flashed
– this taken from me!
No way!
Nothing will stop me
taking this worthless old womb
with me!

And I went to find a book
on hysterectomy.

(Around this time
she learnt to journey
other-wise
met on the way
a large but gentle moose
that nibbled the crunchy growths in her belly
munching them contentedly
like food.
Moose medicine, they said, was self-esteem,
found in Elders who have walked
the Good Red Road.....)

Pauline Rignall

Scorpio

I was born
at this snapping point
of the year

when October winds have ripped
the last rags from the trees
and foam is forced to fly hysterically
across the beach
away from frantic seas

as sparks spiral wildly from our fires
the phoenix spirit soars

I was born
at this snapping point
of the year

I feed the dangerous fires
and feel the fear

I feed the dangerous fires
and feel the fear

(Used as a chant at Samhain)

Dancing in a Place of Power

I step onto a silent stage
an airy space above the stretching sea
strong boards, new wedged
take all the weight
take all the weight of me
beneath the mountains
and above the stretching sea

beyond, steam veils the morning-watered furrows
of compost quickening
in the crumbly earth

a yeasty brewing stirs
in the sticky dough of me
pulls in the leavening air
to lift the limbs of me
the squat square shape of me
the old straight tracks of me

skin pricks with sweat like fur
I feel the turf of me
tough pads of hands make fists
the roughened rocks in me
hurl a stamping rage
for power snatched from me
the power of growth in me
the space to be in me
the place that gives in me

I lift my eyes and see
steam veiling morning-watered furrows
and oh! that never-ending stretch of sea
the ceaseless sweep of waves
draws great draughts of breath to me
quenching an ancient thirst
till sobs and groans are song of me
streams of tears pour from me
the sweet salt snot of me
the strong long song of me

anchored in the old straight tracks of me
arms wingspun in dance
breaking the postures of apology.

Exorcising

OK Godman
between you and me
enough is enough
I'm letting you go
separating
not saying Goodbye
just got my bearings now
taking some space of my own
standing up, eye to divine eye
you gorgeous hunk

you dazzle me not
Apollo
the more I look
the more I see
like it
like what I see
dancing free
free to like what I see

Yummy
YUMMEE
You
Me

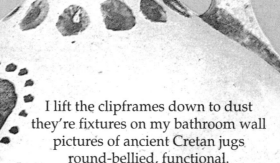

Cretan jugs

I lift the clipframes down to dust
they're fixtures on my bathroom wall
pictures of ancient Cretan jugs
round-bellied, functional.

You could use them to pour milk on your cornflakes.
They could sit on the table,
broody as teapots, soothing, comfortable.
Here's my handle, here's my spout.

And here the painted nipples reach from beaded areolas
as if they would stream into the milky way
and here a neck arches away from the breast
flinging the morning a birdsong: unearthly aria.

And here is her eye, seeking through centuries
making me see. I wipe the glass clean.
Return to the kitchen, make tea.
Yes, I'll be mother. And I am other,

High Priestess of ecstacy.

Pauline Rignall

Following wolf

In this pack I have tracked
and padded and pulled and sometimes
pounced and even
snapped

and been puzzled and paused
sniffed, twitched,
caught the drift
found a way forward
or around.
In this pack I have felt
welcomed and alone
embraced and shunned
powerful and decrepit
infant and ancient.

In this pack I have seen
fellow wolves
smelled their breaths and bodies
known
the stink of fear
pent anger and spent anger
howling grief
roars of sorrow
emptiness
bereavement
pup play
langorous joy.

In this pack I have travelled
in company
through thickets and under open skies
learning to sense
packwise.

Gifted dancer

Mother, you gave me breath
and give it still
fire breath
dragon flame:
let me not waste this strength.

Mother, you gave me rhythm
beat of my heart
drum roll
thunder clap:
let me not waste this love.

Mother, you gave me blood
coursing flow
storm flood
river riot:
let me not waste this freedom.

Mother, you gave me joy
made me Joy God
lightening clouds
mountain peaks:
let me not waste this sight.

Mother, you gave me peace
made me Peace Queen
silence of starry night
satin sea:
let me not waste my wings.

Labyrinth Ritual

The perfume of its skin intoxicates.

She has breathed dust and sharp dry grasses.
She has sore knees and hands
from crawling
breasts hanging to dry earth
along the winding path.

She has taken a bulb
between her teeth
from the dust,
felt its hard promise,
dropped it at the centre,
delivered.

Now teeth
break a different membrane
split wax red taut resistant skin.
Sweet as honey, lime sharp juice
spurts from buttery flesh

and she
is swallowed whole by the apple,
rolled in pleasure's mouth
drunk on her back
ravenous.

On the outward journey
she finds the rattling firesticks
that call up power,
hold spells,
speak from the bones

and takes them to her place in the circle.

Vegetable love

Bleeding, I feed on greens
with carnivorous greed

devour fresh fleshy broccoli spears
– the leafy stalky kind – from the pan.

Ravenous, I pile cress on bread
make spinach soup that looks like liquid moss,

pick peppery rocket from my own back yard,
tear the tender leaves from growing baby beets.

My salivating memory travels far
grasping green meals.

I long for that celery, stringy and dark,
that Greeks braise with their pork

and their grey broad beans
slithering in *avgolemino*

Horta, wild greens of Crete
melting in mounds with garlic and lemon,

broiled zucchini leaves in Calabria
leathery and sweating oil

Egusi soup, slimier than spinach,
swallowed with pounded yams in Africa

callalou soup in Jamaica
champ served with liver in Dublin

while Demeter sternly watches
the alchemies of blood and soil.

Prayer on the sea shore

Let me receive life greedily
swallow like fat spaghetti
the rich ravel of gifts
brought in to me on the tides.

Let me strew my life
like these sea plants
we call weeds
prototypes of intricate crafted things
like lace and filigree
carved ivory
plaited leather thongs
all heaped haphazard
by the affluent ocean
flung on the stones
valueless.

Let me colour my life with contrasts
surf white as the gull's belly
slate grey seas
new blood of unripe blackberries
wine dark womb lining black of bladderwrack
rust and roaring orange
grass green unlikely in this sterile place.

Let me define my life
as this morning the mountains have appeared
cut by scissors, pasted to the sky
shadows outlined in HB pencils.
Let me sweep my beaches clean as these.

Let me hold my life when necessary
in a limpet's limey cloister
with ridged tenacity
but not disabling privacy
holding my truth.

Let me space my life
with time to raise my eyes
to see the bright surf bar
that lifts the felted mountains skywards
from the broken busy sea.

Colour schemes

I hold an Autumn rose
and tread the dangerous Autumn floor
slateslimy, slippery in sunshine,

where whitebeam leaves,
wax yellow and round as plates
are silver as a sweep of rain
from underneath

and red oak leaves drop
deep as cellos
among the timpany of lime and beech.

The glowing ochre of that stone wall
sings under my ribs.

Can't you hear my appetite, fox red,
in that paint on the kitchen door –
a gloss the colour of cuntshine?

Shall we drape wet leaves, calke green,
around our sheets of porphyry pink
and dapple the duvet with misty damson
roughened with russet, speckled with rowan red

and lie under green smoke skies
like Autumn fires
until they die?

Dirty dancing

In partnership with the pampas
grasses sweeping light across the sky

and hydrangea blossom bobbing
like big breasts

and top-heavy rich brown
sunflowers bowing to summer's

final fling, as Equinox gales
smash the light

against metalled yellow petals,
startling the grounded leaves

and thorny elbows of crab apple
jutting towards the dirt

earth-coloured with wrinkled fruit:
promiscuous old dancer.

Broom

They rattled on our shoulders
as we squeezed through summer paths
warning us.

Now broomspit hits us
as the crisp pods split and crackle
splatting their pellets
onto the hot canvas of the afternoon.

Smells of dry dung,
sagebrush, apple mint...
we quiver on the cusp of something
as the sun roars into Leo.

At Imbolc, the graceful arches
of stems were green flames
tense with unlikely life.

We were inspired to trust
these spikes of spring
and placed them on the altar.

By Beltane the burning bush
flaunted red and gold spumes:
as always, ahead of the weather.

Now these bullets oggress us
before we're ready,
but coal black pods curl back
show linings of unpolished gold.

We cut the stuff for broomsticks
for sweeping up the Autumn mess

and for riding through the blankets
to the whitegold deserts
of our winter dreams.

Cold comfort

The morning has a fleece
of frosted grass, each blade as soft as duckdown
with which the souls of my feet
have whispered conversations
about tenderness in dreams
and trusting
and troublesome touch.

In the virtuous snow
my foot reveals a fledgling's flattened skull,
bone threaded triangle
stripped by indifferent winter.

I have lived life sheltered lately,
hooded against the rain
sealed up, sensible...
but my feet on earth
like sparrows' scratch-red legs
still smutch the snow.

I want to dance all day again.
I would let the sun right through me
to raddle me like that duck's body
no longer roundly solid
but fragmented into shards
by broadswords of light
in the bloody, sun-slashed river.

I would risk the fire together
as spring's knives will cut this clean white cover
like a savage lover,
and make love right
though love has been misspelled
and words scratched out
so many times before.

The morning has a fleece
of frosted grass, each blade as soft as duckdown...

Birdwoman 1

Retreating behind curtains
into shadow:
an old face darkly visible.

In the dappled sunlight on the sill
and suspended in air
we glimpse the familiars:
bright arcs, dragonfly green
now seen, now unseen.
They rob us of words,
her legacy of attendant humming birds.

'She had no children' laughs the younger woman
who has learned to play her part,
inviting patiently, birds to visitors,
visitors to birds.
'They are her children.'
We pay the woman Jamaican dollars,
are sat in canvas chairs.

At first they flash like fireflies
in and out of the sun
fierce in flight and fight.
Then closer
a whirr of wings, a breeze, a blur in the air
a slither of silk
and there, on my finger
deep stained and spun like glass
the form precisely wrought.
The beak, no thicker than a thorn,
sips syrup from my hand:
I am become ... a flower!
Bear a near weightlessness
feel faint spider feet...
a presence slipped
from some other place
into an ordinary hour:
a sliver of grace.

Birdwoman 2

Back home the icy wind shoves the door back in my face
rips away the flaps of my dressing gown
as I slither out in slippers
big blobby snow flopping in my face as I throw
seeds on the shed roof
and wet on the back of my neck as I stoop
for the fallen feeder to refill with nuts

retreat back upstairs with the tea tray
into bed and the hot saddle of your back.

We eat our porridge at the window, watching
a wagtail flick his bill all morning at a crust,
daft but determined coal tits hold their own, just,
among their bigger, brightly tailored cousins.
As they feed fast and furious
we become greedy
for the swooping and swerving and jabbing and stabbing
and nibbling and fluttering and fighting...

and from a newly emptied nest, I see
no barren middle age
for birds and beaks and bees still enter me
as you do too, till I feel
through the feathered and fleshed and buzzing and humming
and honeyhoarding eggdropping bloodbearing spermspawning
songspinning
and sparrowdroppings

mere inklings

glinting sometimes
on the narrow sill
of a darkening room

Retiring to the Country

The cockerel that rapes my dreams
over and over
drilled through the open window
where the afternoon had hummed me asleep
in a haze of winey sunshine.
Dogs barked to tear the flesh.
Anna stamped home on concrete, slamming gates
(I was that child once).

I've slunk from the house
like a disgruntled cat
to the woods as evening ripens.

I feel me taking root here
among the warty leafless oaks
my feet like fists in earth, clenching at rocks.

Rocks. Gritty and frowning.
I want to grow my toes around them.
I want them to hold me here
with solid elderly for company

– here, where thin, aspiring spring is overshadowed
(a single stalk of fern
unfurls it's slender length
from the thick thighs of parting roots

and ragged anenomes
droop feeble flakes of white
anaemic on corky bark.)

– and, where bald trees still dance
grisled trunks hold sway
and I have staying power,
am undisturbed.

I smile to think that I will rot like these
decomposing stinking rich with life.

Shore Dancer Returns Home

Bright from the sea
and a sea-visiting company
brought together on the winds

she is lulled as the train
snakes slowly inland
along the Hope Valley.

These homely ruffled hills,
slack valley fields of uncombed grass
wooded mounds made patchy by Autumn:
scrunched oaks, crumbled birches,

are comforting, over-familiar
as her own worn body:
swell of belly, breast weight,
swerve of hip, thighs' big curve.

Boots, rucksack and briefcase bear her down
as she trudges the lane
sees slow smoke drift from home
and then the dog, wafting vaguely by the gate,
humming its gentle recognition
claiming her ...

underskin prickles
at the threat of welcome:
beneath her loosely fitting flesh
and winter clothes

something much tighter, glistening
wet with newness
sleek as the starry night
brushed by a gale

contd

tangy with sea, taste of salt blackberries...
no domestic creature has such skin
since we drove the sacred serpent from our walls –
a black cat comes the closest
but this is cooler, closer, gleams more bright...

Can she fit this shimmering slippery new-self skin
into the warm and faded overcoat of home
without it smudging, rubbing dull?
Can she bear to sort through the debris in those pockets again
brush out the felted dust behind lapels and cuffs
attempt to raise the nap, remove the stains?
Can she smell the sweat of another life
thick around her
and stay this sinewy?
How can she meet him?

She drops her lids on gleaming gems of eyes, feels tired,
is glad of camouflage
as he offers fire and food...
longing to stay awhile where walls are sky-coloured,
changeable and full of mirrors
that reflect her underskin ...
inflame her.

The moon is headlight bright
when she wakes under its glare
having dreamed it was raining
and she on the ground
aroused, snake-naked:
he is not there.

On becoming more than neighbours

We knocked down the fencing
between the terraces
when you came to live next door.
Then we had a door put through
between the living rooms.
The high privet fell:
I bought the electric saw,
and now children run
right round the houses
in open secret passageways.
Dogs' bodies skim the gates.

I sit in a corridor
braced against invasion.
I cannot lie naked in the hammock
or pour my unclothed thoughts
onto the pages
which are caught by the wind
and funnelled through the gaps.

My silences are solid as fortresses though.
I am close as a clam again
and do not feel safe when touched.

I want to buy a smart front door
of hardwood, without windows
and have a peephole and a chain as old ladies do.
I want the fences replaced,
by those high palings
you can't see over
high gates at the side of the house
with the bolt on the inside.

The weaving of a gate

you have in mind
a gate of woven willow...

I watch, as the rightness of the thought
drops like a coin through water
into a treasury
on a still well bottom

where in the dappled light
that wavers through water
or wicker work
I see gates as intentions
lifetimes in the making

starting with strands of pliant green
that grow from the heart's moist soil
weaving takes time
follows a tribal pattern
allowing the special twist
of a personal design
each strand multiplies the strength of the others
infinitely...

would we want our hearts' homes
knocked into shape
with nails?

Uses and abuses of windchimes

Like king and queen
in stately home
we have our separate quarters

steps to climb and halls to cross
before I can be furled in your fleece.

Trapped in so much space
we develop contraptions:
strings tied to wind chimes
my window to yours
to tug should I desire you...

All this to avoid
the marriage I cannot desire:
the homely exposure
of daily, nightly intimacy
resisted with uncomely ferocity.

I used to cart my life around in plastic bags
because I would not be a part of you
and still
I will undress
change a tampon
brush my teeth
shit
in private.

It may be my hangup, but
there is something appealing in the boudoir (or temple) scene
where the mistress (or priestess) appears in full sail
no loose rigging
her nakedness richly adorned.

You too have sometimes appeared to me changed,
exotic, inviting ...

So I cannot be your windchime
always ready for you to brush against.
I need a hideaway,
a den or cave
to find my own tunes.

I do not even want a doorbell.
I'll come out when I'm ready
... or ring you.

Wedding Ring

because I have been smoothed
by your stubborn returning
– yours are the arms that would not go away –
changed by this deep entering
my rocks licked by your trust.

this ring ties no knots
fixes nothing
does not make two into one

its parts are separate,
but married together
as the sea belongs to the shore
meeting in a thousand dances
greeting each other in every mood
merging yet always separating
and governed by the rhythms of a higher She
they keep a bright integrity:
there's space
between the brushed gold beach
and the crystal studded sea.

Forty third spring

Frantic with air freight, the usual morning
fizzes with bird busy-ness
birth business.

Overdue rain in the night stained the deep soil
rootlings can stretch and drink
seed leaves uncurl.

Relentless the blood aches from the shrinking womb
thrums on the slackening drum
of skin sagging dully.

Dark clouds still hang like a hen
on this cold clutch of spring.
Day 29. Unhatched. Infertile.

Pauline Rignall

Borrowed Grace

Clumsy in snorkel and flippers
that drag on the sand until I'm afloat
when breasts and belly hang weightless:
the water lending grace that's not our own
to our white bodies floating like distorted moons
through liquid skies that deepen
from radiant blue through twilight jade to indigo
as the sea-bed suddenly shelves.

I watch an octopus shift under its stone,
puff sand, twitch a tentacle,
then drift to where the ocean has no floor
and the clear darkness is alight
with multitudes of gold-green, nib-sized fish.
Somewhere down there I suspend my disbelief
receive the message emerging from this deep,
written on white tampons, unstained as the moon turned:

somewhere in me was a sea
large enough for a shoal to swim in
a sea-bed safe enough to sink in
send out tentacles and feed.

August 1992

Petal child

There is no way
there is no right way
we have not been taught
any way of being
with this
have no hammock of belief
to lie back in
no sustaining truth
to feed us in this wilderness of loss.

We have no rites passed down
for your passing on
can only listen to what our hearts invent
allow all our hearts to invent
from their love and grief
each in our own way
for all of us.

But after the days of womanly waiting
the still ache of unknowing
the suspension of active life
in the blank ignorance of daylight
while inside life and death
held secret conference

and after my night of untimely labour
when the body decreed
I must use my ancient knowledge
of birth breathing
against the painful spasms
that leave no room for doubt,

when I have no choice but to co-operate
in freeing you
from the greedy embrace of my flesh
our flesh
life's playtime from eternity

when you, the closest
of all lives to me
are already leaving me
before we've met
gone on ahead...

you linger awhile in the ether
dandled in my trance of love
dancing with your company of souls
one new petal brighter than the many
shining your good bye
waving God by me
to comfort me
you comfort me
oh my daughter.

20 September 1992

Part of October's dying

On the palm of my hand at last
a small dark stigma
half the length of my thumb.

Some unspoken, unwritten, unheard of taboo
had held back my hand with the scissors:
I'd broken through.

This chunk of fibrous livery stuff
contained your face. Or not.
I had to know.

Floated in a saucer of water
your pale cowl draped around you
we see you clearly:

Half the length of my thumb.
No limbs. But infinitisemal shadows
mark your eyes.

We stare at you all day.
Three selves in one
woven together in unbounded love.

He weaves you a hand-sized casket
from sweetgrass and straw.
We fill it with rosemary and heartsease. No rue.

What shall I say of the ship she made
of rushes, and sails of white roses,
with miniature dishes of seeds, to take you away?

What of the poems that flowed
from that circle of friends
and the songs we re-wrote for ourselves?

And the cakes that were bought
and the cackling and jokes over tea
'I'll be mother' I say as I pour.

Your spirit had somehow put stars in our hair.
Each May, forget-me-nots crowd your ring of stones, self-seeded,
and we have been rich in missing you for another year.

Freed Dance

able to be different
real different
with me   with you
no struggle
no reacting
just   curious   responding
being   in touch
yes   we are
mirroring true

this is new
no judgement   passing
here I am   whole
not swept into that grief
this rebellion
that up   this down
your trip   her grip
say no   say yes
let the body lead
let the spirit move   the body
how I LOVE this my body
my old brand new sparkling
vital tired
bouncing stretching suffering swaying
explosive
boundingly beautiful body of me
bonded to spirit bones
braced and brave
and free

oh Liberty
oh Liberty

small spirit by my ear
reminding me
reminding me

my baby.

18 October 1992

Elder Mother

I have cut the dead spongy twigs
from the mossy elder
in the shady bottom of the garden.

Little grows here
except this death-divining, wine-producing tree.

Only a lily's glossy leaves uncurl
and the white currants on the fence
dribble dingy strings of flowers.

But I feel a place of dreaming here
a place to take authority
with a clean gnowing.

I stand with my back to the tree, secateurs in hand,
see the spiral of stones that unfurled for me last week
opening our unborn daughter's circle grave.

I will sow violets among the stones
I have stopped believing I cannot do this.

Nothing is so clean as that
which comes straight from the soil
or the body.

No child will stream from me now
but here in my clay-weighed boots
holding a split clod of snowdrop bulbs
between my hands

I am unpeeled
like the whiteness beneath their skin
that gleams through the dirt as brilliant as winter.

Revelation

I touch the wrinkled slack
cobweb soft
tenderly.

It's what we do
to test the setting point of jam:

when the surface crinkles
we remove it from the heat
at once.

Left any longer
it would stiffen and spoil
lose its fresh flavour.

Firm fresh flesh
cannot be bottled and sealed.

The chemistry
that has secretly detached
this flimsy skin from my inner elbow
– revealed as I crook my arm in dance –
cannot be arrested.

I must wither
dance as I may:
movement only reveals me.

The Strength of Cups

1 Full

I am the deep-cupped bloom,
called dranculus, dragon arum
or, commonly, stinkhorn.

I rise waist-high in Crete's May heat
open a crimson throat as long as your arm
to hold you in my wine-dark centre

my sparkling sailor of the wine-dark seas
my man behind the mast
my mast, my thick stamen

I draw you into where there is no space
only the strength of desire to be filled:
(a strength I find no name for
in my Thesaurus)
that seals us both hermetically to pleasure –
Hermes and Aphrodite
become one flame.

The Strength of Cups

2 Minoan

The strength I find no name for
in my Thesaurus
I see was celebrated here
in the sacral knot
the spiralled pot
the snakes that slither and glide
the octopus that clasps and sucks

where the throat of the crocus,
the mouth of the cave,
are invitations to enter
the labyrinth's path
be drawn in
sweet body of the dark
to source the scent...

of a woman stood taut-waisted
breath drawn up, chest filled with fire,
bare breasts flared:
holder of power
holding
golden serpents
arched from her arms
arched upwards
poised: the power of poise
not pounce
it is the power of holding
not the strike
not the strength of the sword
held high, but of cups
hand moulded

of baked earth
strong with the heat of the sun
and great bellied jugs
strong bellied
breasted
strong bodied
beaked
the body thus strong
supports the voice
the voice rises
gives song to the stars
and all is held
in a strong web
a strong fine web
finely designed
hand made
divine.

The Strength of Cups

3 Broken

The limpet hold tightens when knocked
the baby's jaw locks fiercely on the nipple
the lingham is anchored
where the depth cannot be fathomed
and currents draw from the core.

You can't just pull it like a carrot from the ground.
We cannot be untied by banging on the door.

Somehow we surface like whales, call out
but the banging goes on.
Prised apart to show its secret
a fist hits out
'Fuck off!' I shout.

'Do you want this 'phone call or not?'

We should make velvet tasseled cords
strung with silver hearts
to hang across our doors....risk ribaldry.

Sitting at breakfast, words wore suits:
'I don't appreciate being told to f--- off!'

A hurt that will not speak its name
dons uniform
the hammer falls on the bargain
I lose
retreat to my room like a woman
to weep.

We both apologise
we laugh and hug.

All day grief seems to bruise an inner skin.

The Strength of Cups

4 Empty

All day grief seems to bruise an inner skin
though we eat lunch at the harbour
expensively, off starched white linen:
the milky flesh of to-day's catch
with soft poached vegetables and cold white wine.

We return to the mountain
to look for the purse we'd lost.

Yesterday's irises are shrivelled and black
like inky pellets boys threw in school.
The sullen little goatherd at the cross roads
scowls past us as if the road were empty.

Climbing the tall, locked gates to the ruins of Lato,
my skin is spiked with the thrill of forbidden entry.
I retrace the meander of walls and steps
to the silent, sacral court, empty of purses.

The afternoon fizzes and crackles...
cleansing, leavening fire burns out the hurt
leaving – nothing – a vacuum of years
clean stones, a distant view of the sea.

The Strength of Cups

5 Mending

Perhaps we should make velvet tasseled cords
strung with silver hearts
to hang across our stairs

she thought, when the train had gone.
Her shoulders had grown barbs
at the tread of his boots mounting stairs
his big coat filling her doorway
in his haste to talk
– emails and aggravation

(allied planes are screaming
through what were ordinary lives)

The fibres connecting
flimsy fading dreams
with the frosty blossom in the garden:
tear like cobwebs ...
and a different poem gets written.

There have been so many uninvited entries.
Real healing takes many generations.

(the men marched off
all the women in the village raped)

No man can compose
with a pram in the hall
she once heard
– or words to that effect.
And so the canon has been built.

She asks herself again:
in what part of my house do I live?
Where can I find the language
that wounds neither him nor me?
Must I reproduce the violence?

Only she knows his going to work out there
allows her coming to work in here
– Medusa detangling her hair.

Man Dances

You demonstrate the iron musculature
of arms, shoulder, back
used to imitating a fork lift truck
or JCB. We laugh.
See you moving mountains
God never meant to be there,
holding the world on your shoulders.

Dancing, you seem
to slip and slide
among the different elements

flowing and flapping and flailing
with alarming bursts of energy
as joints loosen
limbs test liberty

real easy
now
releasing
delicacy

chest and belly slacken
like a quivering sail
tacking and turning
re-turning, bellied with breath,

taut with it... soft power... dynamite...

Breathdance

He breathes his songs through a short reed pipe.
There is no knowing
What is his voice, and what the sound of the pipe.

"We don't have a word for music
in our language.
Music is the same as life.
We don't speak of playing the mbira,"
(stroking the silver keys as voices fill the air)
"We touch its sounds.
Now, I like you to sing with me.
Na tonde wa. It means I love you.
We sing it to our children.
No, not like that. We sing it with a smile."

He does not smile, he is smiled,
and the light shines from us all.

I am drawn to a space on the ground
danced by the songs
and the big moving airs of morning.

For Frances Bebey, Womad, 1995.

Djembe lessons on Barra Beach

Plaited ropes of rhythm rise
like smoke from a furnace of sound
fanned by a blurr of hands
to the stretched skin of the sky
snake black, brimful of stars.

Facing this same southern reach
of the Atlantic
that suffered the crossing
of manacled griots in slaveships

we fumble on the drumskins
of our pilgrimage
humbled by our teachers
hand servants to the beat

who chisel the tawny mango wood
in the mornings,
stretch the goatskins
test the tautened strings

and smiling
fan the flames
in the veins of night,
with batwing hands
showering the skies
with the gifts of the loose-limbed Gods
that no one succeeded in stealing.

After the lesson,
flakes of smoked fish
wth sour tomato, starchy bits of yam
are flicked our way
in the communal rice bowl:

we learn to eat with our hands again,
are taught the etiquette
of sharing.

Determination

Stupid with instinct,
they have soared from Africa
braving Atlantic rages
to reach this growing grass
in these particular fields.
Secretly, each builds a separate nest
and the young crops hide them.

All along the homeward winding lanes
courting couples on spring nights have thrilled
to the unmusical compelling call
of the corncrake's grating mating cry
that caught the blood in its rush
hushed them,
hands over mouths crushing each other's laughs.

No tractors have till now disturbed the peace
of these rough western reaches
but this year farmers ride on thrones
above the giving soil
and they take an earlier harvest.

Determined still
in this most deadly cyclone
the stubborn mothers
brave a deafening circle closing in
and will not leave their nests
before the eggs have cracked
and hatchlings fled.

Anyone could see them now
who chose to look
as stalks collapse around them

but the beating blades of the harvester
has sliced them through
like meat for bread

and feathers are floating
above where the hens have bled.

flown

no birds fly
in this killing wind
not even driftwood
worn by brutal loving
has been left by these waves

the beach is a cold desert
all debris buried by the frenzied sand

except for this thing
becalmed in the storm
its long black flight feathers
still trying to flap
helpless under the wind's taunts

the whole frame is intact
bird bones like fine china clean and thin
bird's fish-eating flesh all gone
bird's fish-seeking eyesockets empty
bird's wailing call of the sea drowned
birdribs a perfect cage
unbroken
wide open
to the wind's breath

Aftermath

Spraying the trays
of embryos
all green with hope

tucked up in the glasshouse:
where air is moist and warm
as children's breath, asleep,

I savour the subtle
defensive designs
of the separate species:

satin sweet basil
has two smooth lobes turned back
to form a perfect shield

lady's bedstraw lies flat on the earth
while friesia forces blades up
stiff and sharp

brussel sprouts ooze from the soil
like wormcasts wearing
seedskins as skull caps

against the weather,
which suddenly, outrageously,
pours down the valley

like smoke,
and hailstones rattle
like bullets on the glass

leaving a layer of ice
on April's face
unreal as television pictures

of infant human mouths
designed to root and suck
gone dry

of baby fingers reaching for support
like sweet peas' feeble tendrils
withering.

In warm rooms, we'd watched our glass screen:
hands lay pale, fish-shaped parcels
of newborn babies, weightless as lettuce seeds

on bare mountains
in trenches of snow
as if they might grow.

April 1991. (During the Iraq War)

Man against nature

He came without my noticing at first
although by prior arrangement
and set about his work
as unobtrusively as rivers stack up silt.

I see him sometimes treading down my path
unhurried as winter
in this soothing, warm November.

And so the broken wall
is put apart
the stones arranged in piles by size
then layer by layer
in imitation of geology
their massive weight is packed up solidly again
squared firm around the tree
whose swaying trunk in last November's storm
had brought it down

let in fox havoc
left Mary, the six year old maran
stone heavy without her head
among the squabble of her children's corpses.
Only the blue-black aracuna, wings unclipped
escaped into the night.

We buried all the bodies but the youngest
which we braced ourselves
to try to pluck and gut.
Next door's children – vegetarians –
watched wide-eyed
as scarlet tubes
and tiny amber egg yolks flecked with red
were tenderly delivered into light.

Hallowe'en is past now
children are squealing home along the lane
from night's vague fingers straying into day

while the stone man stands quietly by the gate
this evening, waiting for his mate
to help him lift the cope stones into place.

Ways of being

way mislaid
wet woods mistladen
water colourless
afternoon walk

from a sunken meadow
between the merging rivers
three ducks
startle
a sudden tangent
towards

a smudge of gold
glowing
on plum-bloom cloud.

Footsteps deliberate as bricks
from behind a wall.
Men's voices.
'Definitely, yes, definitely,'
one says
not noticing

a smudge of gold
on plum-bloom cloud
fading.

Stone circle

There were paths and then there were roads.
They make roads for the likes of us to use.
We have to use them to get to some place else
we've decided to go.

But paths are what we find
when we may not have somewhere in mind
to get to.
We don't always know
why we choose them,
often we think we lose them.

There's no sign of a path now
to lead to the circle of stones.
Only sheep tracks lead us around
and around
till we find them

the broken stones
licked by the warm tongue of time
have been worn down smooth,
almost part of the ground.

We sit
uncertain of ourselves,
our paths, our ways,

while over there,
across the sunsoaked moors
the road roars by
lorries to quarries
steel to smash stone
sound that slices silence
like an alarm.

Someone starts us humming.

Communion

We knew they were only sheeptracks
but as the guidebook passed from hand to hand
we had quickly lost the path

– had we started at the wrong church?

So we followed the lie of the land
creased like the palm of a cupped hand
revealing these lifelines

– paths unspooling like thread
through the pass just ahead, the next step
feeling almost familiar

to the four of us, cheerfully
reminding each other of the names of flowers:
varieties of vetch, I would always forget,

you stumbled on asphodel
(Anastasia, Artemisia, Adrasteia,
all came out instead!)

But then we emerged where their wide-frocked stems
steepled a fairy forest on a strand of scattered stones.
'Asphodel grow on cemeteries,' I said.

'To feed the spirits of the dead,' you read.
We took it in, a role reversal
that could change your view of life, and death.

'The stalks are edible fried
the seeds can be roasted
best of all are the roots cut up with figs.'

Standing together in that breezy, bare-rock place
swept over by the stone-washed sheets of sky
we nibbled the nutty petals

thoughtfully as chefs,
tasting recipes for spirit guests.

Marrowstone Island

we'e travelled America
and reached a kind of edge
a finger pointing northwards on the map

driftwood rims the beaches
embracing inner seas
like upstretched arms
knuckles and longbones
bare
abstracts of cellular complexity
shadow shapes distilling
mystery

here
movement is held by stillness
slow sunsets and
heron stand
at dawn
awaiting the tide's rising
that's all

and then I hear
a voice I know
music made of rain and snow
a beating heart beneath the bone
pulse in the stone

out of the pain of all passing
sinew of rhythm

prayers for the living

For Jai Uttal.

Under Mt Shasta

I could come clean
living in this lake-water

just floating naked,
towards the sacred mountain.

Could grow old
here, suspended in silence.

Words would rise sparely
from the depths of me.

A pattern might sometimes
like this breeze silvering the surface

cause someone's skin to shiver
or like a fish on a line

the flashing life of a phrase
might arrest a breath

or my toe in the sand might startle a crab-
like habit of mind.